Debbie and Randy Coe

Schiffer Publishing Ltd ®

4880 Lower Valley Road, Atglen, PA 19310 US

Title page photo:
Top Left: Elephant; **Top Right**: Wolf/Swan; **Center**: Bull; **Bottom Left**: Cat; **Bottom Center**: Dog; **Bottom Right**: Cow

Debbie and Randy Coe are authors of the following books:

Elegant Glass: Early, Depression & Beyond
Liberty Blue Dinnerware
Glass Animals & Figurines
Avon's 1876 Cape Cod Collection Glass Dinnerware
Fenton Burmese Glass
Fenton Basket Patterns- Acanthus to Hummingbird
Fenton Basket Patterns- Innovation to Wisteria & Numbers

Published by Schiffer Publishing Ltd.
4880 Lower Valley Road
Atglen, PA 19310
Phone: (610) 593-1777; Fax: (610) 593-2002
E-mail: Info@schifferbooks.com
For the largest selection of fine reference books on this and related subjects,
please visit our web site at **www.schifferbooks.com**
We are always looking for people to write books on new and related subjects. If
you have an idea for a book please contact us at the above address.
This book may be purchased from the publisher.
Include $3.95 for shipping.
Please try your bookstore first.
You may write for a free catalog.
In Europe, Schiffer books are distributed by
Bushwood Books
6 Marksbury Ave.
Kew Gardens
Surrey TW9 4JF England
Phone: 44 (0) 20 8392-8585; Fax: 44 (0) 20 8392-9876
E-mail: info@bushwoodbooks.co.uk
Free postage in the U.K., Europe; air mail at cost.

Library of Congress Control Number: 2005937703

Designed by Mark David Bowyer
Type set in Seagull Hv BT / Souvenir Lt BT

ISBN: 0-7643-2385-7
Printed in China
1 2 3 4

Contents

Dedication

We dedicate this book to all the considerate volunteers worldwide who work so hard to make sure animals are well cared for and have good homes. Long hours are spent ensuring that animals will have a better life. There are so many dedicated animal organizations, such as the Humane Society and People for Ethical Treatment of Animals (PETA), who work to aid and protect animals. In addition, zoos and animal sanctuaries around the world work towards the improvement of life for animals. We applaud all their efforts in addressing the needs of all these animals.

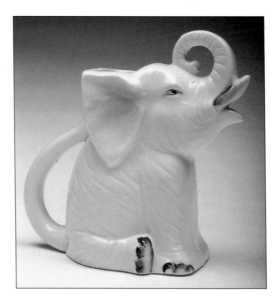

Acknowledgments

Each of our children, Myra & Stephen Hixson and Tara & Jeff McRitchie, shared the animal pitchers from their respective elephant and cat collections for this book. We appreciate their contributions.

Cricket and Gary Propp, who live with many of these special animals, graciously allowed us to photograph their collection. We really appreciate them being part of this project.

In addition, we are indebted to the Lafayette Schoolhouse Antique Mall in Lafayette, Oregon, for allowing us to make photographs of many of the different animals there. We talked with several of the customers who shared information about their collections of animal pitchers. Some were collecting only cows, while others only wanted unusual animals. This type of collection appeals to a great many different collectors.

Top Left: Bird
Top Center: Sheep
Top Right: Duck
Center: Elephant
Bottom Left: Dog
Bottom Center: Turtle

Introduction

In the past couple of years, as advisors to several price guides, we have become aware that cute, small, figural pitchers in the shapes of animals have attracted new followers. They are still easy to find and most are reasonably priced.

These animals have been made by many different American ceramic and pottery companies, including American Bisque, Blue Ridge, Brayton Laguna, Fitz & Floyd, Hull, Lenox, McCoy, Rio Hondo Potteries, Shawnee, Spaulding China with their Royal Copley line, Stewart Ceramics, and Vallona Starr. They also come from Japan and Germany, as well as Bavaria, China, Czechoslovakia, England, France, Holland, Italy, Mexico, Occupied Japan, and Taiwan.

Opposite Page:
Top Left: Pig; **Top Right**: Chicken
Center: Lion; **Bottom Left**: Chicken
Bottom: Center: Cow; **Bottom Right**: Pheasant

Animal pitchers were produced for many years to provide interesting and decorative items for use on the table. Many were produced as souvenir items and sometimes can be found with place names marked on them. At antiques malls and shows, an assortment usually can be found. As one might expect, cow pitchers are the most common and exotic animals are the hardest to find.

We think this will be a fun and interesting book for all the different collectors who love and collect animals and their related items. We hope you enjoy this large assortment.

Measurements

Actual height and width measurements were taken for each pitcher as it was photographed. We measured the tallest part and the longest parts of every piece. When the shape was irregular, the larger measurement was used. Many pitchers are found in more than one size. In some instances a creamer can be found with a matching water pitcher.

Values Guide

All the values given in this book are for pitchers in **Mint Condition** only. Any type of damage, such as a chip or crack, will greatly diminish the value. Pieces that have been repaired should reflect a far below normal value, depending on their appearance.

We have asked both collectors and dealers to contribute values so we could obtain a true reflection of the current market. The listed values have been derived from actual dealer sales, what collectors have paid, prices seen at shows, auction results and national publications. As with any type of collectible, there are some regional differences in supply and demand.

A collector ultimately needs to decide what he would be willing pay for a specific item. Our job is to report the prices that were found, not to set values based on our opinions. This book is to be used only as guide when determining what an item is worth, based on available information.

Neither, the author or publishers assume any responsibility for transactions that may occur because of this book.

The Animals

Since the beginning of man's existence on earth, we believe animals have been part of life, as companions or a food source. Today, many people live with a bird, cat, or dog as pets. In rural areas, farms have different types of animals, including chickens, cows, ducks, goats, horses, and sheep. Depending on where each of us lives, there are various wild animals in our environment. The beauty of each of these creatures is breathtaking. There are many sanctuaries around the world that show animals that we would not be able to see otherwise. They are a large part of our wonderful existence.

Artists use animals as part of their designs. Many times a designer might work at one company before moving on to another. In addition, they could work at a glass company and then go to a pottery company, or visa-versa. When searching for items to own, you can find similar designs in different mediums. Many times you will find that companies like Royal Bayreuth made wonderful creamers and Japanese companies made less-expensive examples in the same design. You may also find Czechoslovakian creations that have been copied in China today.

The animals presented here came from all over the world and there are artistic differences in them. Some may be realistic while others are quite comical. There are representatives of the animal kingdom as well as fairy tales, and even some dressed in people-style clothing. They are each worthy of your enjoyment and use.

Alligator

The alligator is related to the crocodile and is in the family called *Crocodylidae*. There are two types of alligators; one is from the south eastern part of the United States and the other comes from the Yangtze area of China. They live around lakes, rivers and swamps. The alligator's eyes are set above their head to enable them to remain submerged and yet see above the water level. A sweeping motion of their tail propels them quickly through water. On land, their short feet enable them to travel rapidly across the terrain. For a very short distance, they can outrun most other American animals. Their long and sharp teeth are used to grab and rip their prey. Their usual food source is fish, turtles and rodents. Some have been known to attack dogs and small livestock. A typical male can weigh up to 550 pounds and be 12 feet long. The female forms a nest out of grass and mud. She can lay up to 60 eggs and then covers them up. About 9 weeks later baby alligators emerge. The alligator mother is very caring and watches out for her young for approximately a year.

Only one example of an alligator was found for this book. It will be interesting to see if more surface. We expected to find them because of tourist attractions at places such as The Florida Everglades.

Alligator, Beige with Brown accents, 3.5" tall, 5" long, not marked on bottom, circa 1980s, **$12.50**

Bear

The bear is classified in the Carnivore family, meaning they consume mainly meat. They also eat berries, insects and leaves as part of their diet. There are many types of bears that live in different climates. The largest bear is the Alaska Brown bear. It is 9 feet long and can weigh up to 1700 pounds. The smallest bear is the Sun Bear in Malaysia. This bear is only 4 feet long and weighs about 100 pounds. All bears live in Asia, Europe, North America or South America. While odd, no bears can be found in either Africa, Antarctica or Australia.

The bear seems to be a creature that was not used for pitchers very often. *The Three Bears* is a favorite children's story. The bear has always been a Native American symbol of strength.

Bear, Greenish Brown with White chest, 3.5" tall, 4" long, not marked on bottom, circa 1960s, **$9.50**

Bear, Brown, wearing a bow tie, 4.75" tall, 3.5" long, marked on bottom "© Otagiri, Japan, " circa 1960s, **$7.50**

Bird

Birds can be found all over the world in a wide variety of climates. There are over 9,700 types of birds. They belong to the Vertebrae family and are warm-blooded, like mammals. They have feathers that enable them to soar through the sky. The smallest bird is the Bee Hummingbird that is 2" long. The largest bird is the Ostrich that can grow to be 8 feet tall. Birds reproduce by laying eggs in a nest. One or both parents can help incubate the eggs. Typically the young are taken care of until they learn to fly and can feed themselves, which is usually a few months. Man has long been fascinated by a bird's ability to fly and birds have served as important symbols in different cultures.

With a vast variety of bird pitchers to choose from, we were able to assemble a fun chapter. Because designers like taking some artistic license, it is almost impossible to figure out what type of bird some may represent. The Kingfisher and tropical varieties happen to be some of the most popular.

Bird, Snow, Turquoise with Gold accents, 4" tall, 4.5" long, marked on bottom: "Valona Pat 54 Bird Starr," Made by Vallona Starr, circa 1950s, **$19.50**

Bird, Snow, 4" tall, 4.5" long, Made by Vallona Starr, circa 1950s
Left: Light Yellow with Gold accents, **$16.00**
Right: Bright Yellow with Gold accents, **$18.00**

Bird, Toucan, Black with Yellow chest and Orange bill, 9" tall, 10.5" long, not marked on bottom, Made in Japan, circa 1980s, **$12.00**

Bird, Kingfisher, Pink and Yellow with Brown accents, 5.75" tall, 5.5" long, marked on bottom: "Stewart ©", circa 1940s and 1950s, **$19.50**

Bird, Kingfisher, Blue with Pink bill and chest, Green wings and handle, 3.2" tall, 4.5" long, marked on bottom: "Made in England", circa 1930s, **$14.50**

Bird, Kingfisher, Green luster with Orange bill, Blue top of head, Brown base, Black wings, 3" tall, 3" long, not marked on bottom, Made in Japan, circa 1930s, **$12.50**

Bird, Kingfisher, Turquoise with Orange beak, Green, Red and Blue wings, 6.25" tall, 6" long, marked on bottom in Black: "Japan", circa 1930s, **$12.50**

Bird, White with Orange bill and Blue head, Gold wings, Luster finish, 4" tall, 5" long, marked on bottom: "Made in Japan", circa 1930s, **$18.50**

Bird, Mardi Gras style, Ladies face underneath beak, Yellow head and feet, Green top wings, Orange lower feathers, 4.75" tall, 6.5" long, marked on bottom in Black: "Germany", circa 1920s, **$85.00**

Bird, Pelican, Yellow and Blue body, Reddish Brown bill, Blue handle, 3" tall, 3.5" long, marked on bottom in Red: "Japan", circa 1920s, **$16.00**

Bird, Parrot, Orange with Brown accents, Gray beak and feet, 3.75" tall, 3.5" long, marked on bottom in Black: "Japan", circa 1930s, **$19.50**

Opposite Page:
Bird, Left: Crow, Black with Red eyes, 1.25" tall, 1.5" long, not marked on bottom, circa 1950s, **$4.50**
Right: Parrot, Turquoise top, Yellow and Green bottom, not marked on bottom, circa 1950s, **$5.00**

Bird. Left: Parrot, Brown, 4.25" tall, 4" long, not marked on bottom, circa 1940s and 1950s, **$9.50**
Right: Parrot, Yellow, 4.5" tall, 4.25" long, marked on bottom in Black: "Made in Japan", circa 1930s, **$12.50**

Bird, Parrot. **Left:** White with Yellow and Green, 4" tall, 5" long, marked on bottom in Black: "Hand painted Takahashi San Francisco", circa 1960s, **$7.50**
Right: Pink with Turquoise and Green accents, 3.5" tall, 5" long, marked on bottom in Black: "Monterey California", circa 1940s and 1950s, **$12.50**

Bird, Green and Blue back with Orange front, Black bill, 4.75" tall, 3.5" wide, marked on the bottom in Red: "Germany", circa 1920s, **$28.00**

Bird, White with Gold accents and Orange flower, 4.75" tall, 4.75" long, not marked on bottom, circa 1940s, **$24.50**

Bunny

The bunny, or rabbit, is part of the Genera group. They are mammals that feed on fruits, grains and grasses and can be found all over the world. The Cottontail is the most common. Bunnies serve many purposes. They are used in laboratories for research, for meat and fur sources, and as pets. In the wild, a bunny can live only to about 6 years, but pets can live to be 12 years old. During the day bunnies usually sleep but are active at night.

In many children's stories, bunnies are used as a favorite character. Beatrix Potter used Peter Rabbit in some of her tales. Bugs Bunny is a favorite Warner Bros. cartoon character. Disney Studios used Roger Rabbit in their full-length movie production.

Here, we find both bunnies and rabbits depicted as realistic and imaginative. They are quite the assortment.

Bunny, White with Pink bow and Green leaf handle, 8.25" tall, 6.25" long, marked on bottom in Black: "Hand Painted Takahashi San Francisco", also has a Gold foil label that says: "Takahashi San Francisco 94103 Made in Japan", circa 1970s, **$19.50**

Bunny, White with Pink spots, 4.5" tall, 5" long, marked on bottom: "Schmid Design Lolio TM hand painted", Made in Japan, circa 1960s, **$12.50**

Bunny, White with Pink ears and nose, 4.5" tall, 4.5" long, marked on bottom: "Japan", circa 1970s, $**8.50**

Opposite Page:
Bunny, White with Yellow flower decals, Pink ears, 3.5" tall, 6" long, marked on bottom: Red and Gold foil label says "Original Lenwile Ardalt Artware Japan", circa 1970s, **$12.00**

Bunny, White, Has a hat and bow tie, 6" tall, 5.5" long, not marked on bottom, circa 1940s, **$14.50**

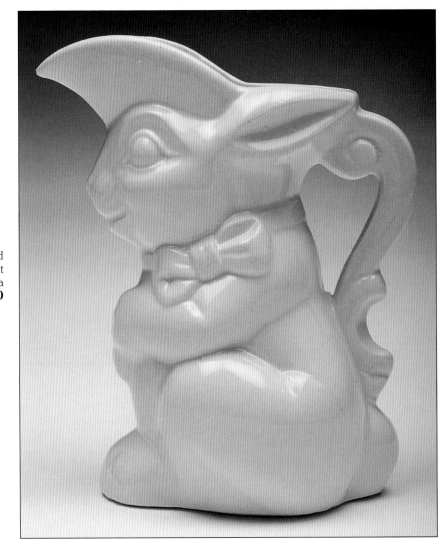

Bunny, White with Blue flowers, 4.5" tall, 4" long, not marked on bottom, Made in Japan, circa 1970s, **$12.50**

Cat

While cats have been living for about 40 million years, they were first domesticated by the Egyptians around 3500BC. Egyptians worshiped a goddess of love and fertility, who was represented by a woman with a cat's head. Cats held such high prominence that if you killed one, you could be punished by death. They were also mummified with their owners. The ancient Greeks held cats in high regard because of their ability to rid an area of rodents.

The domestic cat is listed as *Felis Domesticus*. In the United States, the Cat Fanciers Association recognizes 24 short-hair breeds and 13 long-hair breeds. A favorite pet around the world is the cat. Domestic cats as well as wild ones have often been a favorite of artisans choosing subjects for creamers. Cat collectors have helped to drive up the prices a little. One reason for this is that cat collectors usually collect all types of cats, while dog collectors usually collect specifically by the breed.

The cat is another favorite of storytellers. *Puss in Boots* and *The Cat in the Hat* are some entertaining stories for children. Disney Studios has used cats in many of their movies. Some of the favorites are *Aristocats*, *Lady and the Tramp* with the wicked cats of Si and Am, *That Darn Cat*, and *Winnie the Pooh* with Tigger. An older cartoon character was Felix, and later cats were thrust into public attention by the cartoon *Garfield*.

Opposite Page:
Cat, Brown and Gold floral patchwork, Yellow bow around neck, 6.25" tall, 6" long, not marked on bottom, Made by Brayton Laguna, circa 1940s, **$75.00**

35

Cat, White with Blue tie, 4.75" tall, 4" long, marked on bottom: "Tony Wood Studio England", circa 1930s, **$19.50**

Cat, Beige with Pink and Blue flowers, Orange with Yellow polka dot bow, 3.5" tall, 5" long, not marked on bottom, Made in Korea, circa 1990s, **$8.50**

Cat, White with Blue flowers, Light Blue bow and ribbon around neck, 5" tall, 5" long, not marked on bottom, Made in Japan, circa 1970s, **$14.50**

Cat, Dark Gray with White face and boots, 7.1" tall, 7" long, marked on bottom: "Pretty Kitty", Made by Seymour Mann, circa 1990, **$18.50**

Cat, White and Black, Red bow, 5" tall, 5.25" long, not marked on bottom, Made in Japan, circa 1930s, **$18.00**

Cat, Brown and White, Pink bow around neck, Pink accents inside ears, 4" tall, 5" long, marked on bottom with Gold foil label: "Hand Painted Pacific Japan", circa 1950s, **$12.00**

Cat, Black with Green eyes, 5.5" tall, 5.5" wide, not marked on bottom, Made in Japan, circa 1950s, **$18.00**

Cat. Left: Black and White, 4.5" tall, 5.5" long, not marked on bottom, circa 1960s, **$12.00**
Right: Black and White, 4.5" tall, 7.5" long, marked on bottom: "© Sigma the Taste Setter
Made in Korea", circa 1990s, **$9.50**

Cat, White with Green accents, Pink bow, 3.5" tall, 3.5" long, marked on bottom in dark Green: "Japan", circa 1950s, **$9.50**

Opposite page:
Cat. Left: White, 4.5" tall, 4" long, marked on bottom, "Made in Japan", circa 1980s, **$6.50**
Right: Black and White, 4.25" tall, 4.5" long, marked on bottom with Gold and Black foil label: "SC Seven Corporation" and another Gold and Red foil label that says: "Made in Japan", circa 1970s, **$12.50**

Cat, White with Red bow, Blue accents, 4.75" tall, 4.75" long, marked on the bottom: 'Patented Puss n Boots U.S.A.", Made by Shawnee Pottery, circa 1940s, **$39.50**

Chicken

Today's common chicken originated from the wild fowl of China. The chicken was first raised for their colorful feathers and eggs. Later, they were used as a source of meat. When early seafarers sailed across the oceans, they frequently took chickens with them to supply their crew with food. Spanish sailors introduced the chicken to America. The farm family frequently had several types of chicken wandering around.

Worldwide, over 140 billion pounds of chicken meat is consumed in a year. It is a good source of protein that is low in fat. Major chicken farms can be found in the United States, Brazil, China and Mexico.

We are not sure why, with cream being the intended use for many pitchers, but there are many chickens designed as creamers. They are well-suited for a kitchen collectible, and many kitchens bear a chicken motif.

Chicken, Crowing Rooster, Green and Blue with Red and Yellow top feathers, vegetables near feet, 12.25" tall, 9.25" long, marked on bottom in Black: "© Fitz and Floyd China', circa 1990s, **$75.00**

Chicken, Rooster, Yellow and Gray, Red comb, Flowered blanket on back, 9.75" tall, 9.25" long, not marked on bottom, circa 1990s, **$14.00**

Chicken, White with Pink and Green flowers, Yellow beak, Blue comb,
3.25" tall, 3.5" long, not marked on bottom, circa 1990s, **$5.00**

Chicken, 5" tall, 5.5" long, Made by Spaulding China, Royal Copley
line, circa 1940s and 1950s, **$35.00**
Left: Pink, Yellow and Blue; **Right:** Brown, Pink and Yellow

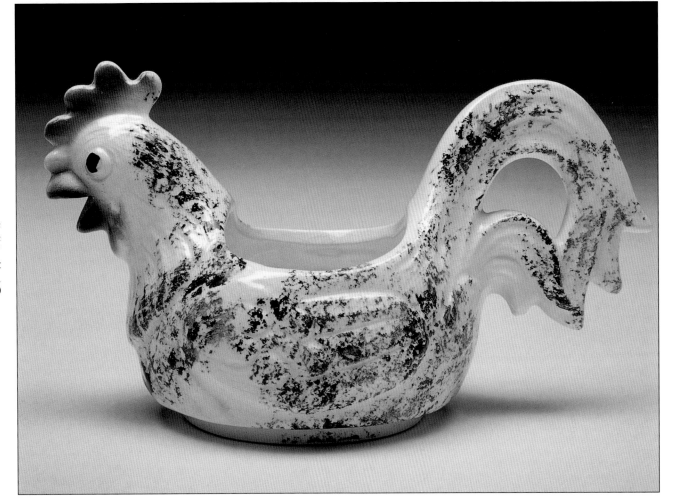

Chicken, White with Black sponge work design, 4" tall, 7" long, not marked on bottom, circa 1970s, **$7.50**

Chicken, Dominique, Black and White all over, Green base, Red comb, 4.75" tall, 4.6" long, not marked on bottom, Made in Japan, circa 1960s, **$14.50**

Chicken, White with Pink flowers, Green top and handle, 5" tall, 7.5" long, not marked on bottom, circa 1980s, **$7.50**

Chicken, White with Pink and Blue flowers, Yellow beak, 5.5" tall, 4.5" long, marked on bottom in Black: "Blue Ridge China Hand painted Underglaze Southern Potteries Inc. Made U.S.A.", in Orange-"Chick Jay #1", circa 1940s, **$85.00**

Chicken, Orange head, Yellow and Green body, Blue beak, salt glaze finish, 3.5" tall, 4.5" long, marked on bottom in black: "Made in Japan", circa 1920s, **$9.50**

Chicken, Gray, Orange head, Pink comb, 3" tall, 5" long, marked on bottom in Black: "Made in Occupied Japan", circa 1945 to 1952, **$12.50**

Chicken, White with Pink flowers and Blue accents, Red comb, Yellow feet, 10.25" tall, 10.5" long, marked on the bottom in Blue: "Poppies on Blue © Lenox", circa 1990s, **$35.00**

Chicken, Brown and Yellow body, Red comb, 9.75" tall, 7.5" long, not marked on bottom, circa 1940s and 1950s, **$24.00**

Chicken, Blue, 4" tall, 5.5" long, not marked on bottom, Made in Japan, circa 1970s, **$12.50**

Chicken, Black with Red comb, Yellow beak and accents on handle, 2.5" tall, 3" long, not marked on bottom, Made in Japan, circa 1950s, **$7.50**

Chicken. Left: Gray and Black, Pink comb, 4" tall, 6" long, not marked on bottom, circa 1960s **$10.00**
Right: Yellow and Brown with Black tail, Red comb, marked on bottom: "Otagiri 1951', Made in Japan, **$18.50**

Chicken. Left: White with Green and Blue drip glaze, Pink comb, 4.25" tall, 5" wide, not marked on bottom, circa 1940s, **$8.50**
Right: White with Brown floral transfer decal, 4.5" tall, 5.75" long, not marked on bottom, circa 1960s, **$7.50**

Chicken, White with Black, 4.5" tall, 6" long, not marked on bottom, circa 1990s, **$6.50**

Chicken. Left: White with Yellow and Green accents, 6.25" tall, 5.5" long, marked on bottom in Black: "Made in Italy", circa 1970s, **$9.50**
Right: Orange, Green, Red and Blue, 6" tall, 5.5" long, marked on bottom in Black: "Heartfelt Kitchen Creations Young's Hand wash only Do not microwave Made in China", circa 1990s, **$9.50**

Chicken. Left: Beige with Blue, Brown and Black accents ,Green base, Red comb, 2.75" tall, 4.5" long, marked on bottom in Blue: "Hand painted Made in Japan", circa 1950s, **$9.50**
Right: White with Orange and Black accents, 4.5" tall, 5.5" long, marked on bottom in Red: "Japan", circa 1950s, **$12.50**

Chicken. **Left:** White with Black accents, Pink comb, 4.25" tall, 4.25" long, not marked on bottom, circa 1980s, **$6.50**
Right: White with Brown accents, Pink comb, 4" tall, 4.5" long, not marked on bottom, circa 1940s, **$6.00**

Chicken. Left: White, 2.75" tall, 4.75" long, marked on bottom in dark Green: "Made in Czechoslovakia", circa 1930s, **$7.50**
Right: Yellow, 4" tall, 7" long, not marked on bottom, circa 1970s, **$8.50**

Chicken. **Left:** Yellow and Green, Pink flower, 3.25" tall, 3.5" long, not marked on bottom, circa 1980s, **$8.50**
Right: Green, 3.5" tall, 2.5" long, not marked on bottom, circa 1990s, **$4.00**

Cow

Cows are in the Bovine family. It is thought that Viking sailors first brought cattle to America. Christopher Columbus's ships also brought cattle on his second voyage to the West Indies. These cattle were then introduced to Mexico and later to Texas. Cattle were important as food sources during the colonizing of America and to the pioneers who made their way West.

Of all the animals raised on a farm, cattle are considered the most valuable. Beef cattle provide meat and dairy cows produce milk that can be used to make butter, cheese, ice cream and yogurt. Cattle are raised worldwide in many climates, from cold Iceland to hot areas of Africa.

The image of a cow as a vessel for cream should be a match made in heaven. Since cow creamers are so plentiful, many pitcher collectors tire of cows unless they are outstanding. The range of cow pitchers that can be found runs from plain to very elaborate and some even depict human traits. Cows are a favorite theme in kitchens. Some cow creamers are found with advertising, having been a souvenir from a certain place.

Cow, Black and White, 5" tall, 7" long, Advertising for Hershey, not marked on bottom, Made in Japan, circa 1960s, **$18.50**

Opposite Page:
Cow, Black and White, Gray horns, nose, tail and hooves, 5" tall, 7" long, not marked on bottom, circa 1970s, **$12.00**

Cow, White with Green parsley on sides and head, 5" tall, 7" long, marked on bottom in Red: "#8276", circa 1980s, **$15.00**

Cow, White with Blue windmill and flowers, Delft style, 3.5" tall, 5.75" long, marked on bottom: "Made in Holland", circa 1960s, **$14.50**

Cow, Black and White, Gray tail tip and feet, 3.5" tall, 5.5" long, paper label says: "Hand Painted Otagiri Japan", marked on bottom: "© Otagiri", circa 1960s, **$8.50**

Cow, Black and White, Blue ribbon around neck with Yellow bell, 4" tall, 5" long, marked on bottom: "B", circa 1970s, **$8.50**

Cow, Black and White, Blue
ribbon around neck, 3.5" tall,
4.5" long, marked on
bottom: "Made in USA",
circa 1940s, **$8.50**

Cow, White with Black spots, Yellow face and horns, Brown hair on top of head, 4.5" tall, 5.5" long, marked on bottom in Black: "Produced for Houston Harvest Gift Products Not recommended for dishwasher or microwave use Franklin Park, Il. 60131 Made in China", circa 1990s, **$7.50**

Cow, Brown, Gray horns and hooves, 4.2" tall, 5.5" long, marked on bottom: "Otagiri 1981", Made in Japan, **$8.50**

Cow, White with dark Brown spots, laying down, Gray horns, Pink nose, 3.25" tall, 6.5" long, marked on bottom in Black: "Block Gear China", circa 1990s, **$6.50**

Cow, White with Blue tulips, Blue hooves, tip of tail, horns and mouth, 4.25" tall, 7.25" long, Cream written on side, marked on bottom in Green: "E-3801", circa 1980s, **$8.50**

Cow, Dark Blue, 5" tall, 7.25" long, marked with Gold foil label: "HIC Japan", circa 1970s, **$14.50**

Cow, White with floral decals on side and Red carnation on head, 4.5" tall, 7" long, marked on bottom in Blue: "Cordon Bleu B.I.A. France", circa 1970s, **$12.00**

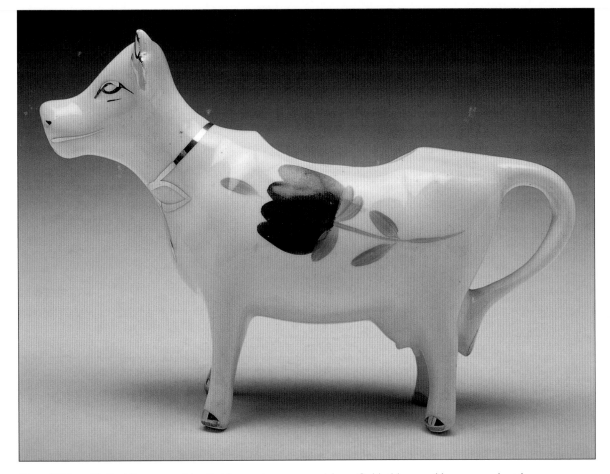

Cow, White with Red flower on side, Gold accent on ears and face, Gold ribbon and bow around neck, 5.25" tall, 7.75" long, not marked on bottom, Made in Japan, circa 1950s, **$14.50**

Cow, head, Orange with Yellow horns, Green interior, 3.75" tall, 5" long, marked on bottom: 'MW Co. hand painted Made in Germany", circa 1920s, **$48.00**

Cow, Brown with White blaze on face, 4" tall, 6.5" long, marked on bottom: "Made in Japan", circa 1950s, **$9.50**

Cow, White with Brown, string tied around neck with metal bell, 3.75" tall, 5.75" long, marked on bottom: a bee inside a V "Made by Goebel", circa late 1940s, **$24.50**

Cow, Brown with dark Brown hooves, 3.25" tall, 5.25" long, marked on bottom: "Japan", circa 1950s, **$14.50**

Cow, Orange with Black tail and horns, 4.5" tall, 5.75" long, marked on bottom: "Made in Czecho-Slovakia", circa 1920s, **$38.50**

Cow, White with Blue windmill and fern prongs on shoulders, 4" tall, 6" long, marked on bottom: "Delft Blue Painted", Made in Holland, circa 1960s, **$12.50**

Cow, White with Brown head, dressed up as a lady with a hat and purse, by her side is a milk can and on her back is a barrel, tail makes the handle, 6.4" tall, 5.25" long, marked along bottom edge: "5079/ 0", Made in Germany, circa 1920s, **$60.00**

Cow, Black and White, 3.75" tall, 5.75" long, not marked on bottom, Made in Japan, circa 1970s, **$9.50**

Cow, White with Purple, Pink and Yellow accents, Blue ribbon around neck, 4.25" tall, 4.75" long, not marked on bottom, Made in Japan, circa 1950s, **$9.50**

Cow, Light Brown with Orange ribbon and Silver bell around neck, 4.25" tall, 3.75" long, marked on the bottom in Red: "Made in Germany", circa 1930s, **$16.50**

Cow, Blue calico flowers, 3.5" tall, 7.25" long, marked on bottom in Blue: "Royal Crownford Ironstone England', also incised with: "1074P", circa 1980s, **$35.00**

Cow, Bull, Black with White chest, Brown horns, Pink ears, 3" tall, 2.5" long, not marked on bottom, Made in Japan, circa 1930s, **$9.50**

Cow, Black and White, Gold collar and bell around neck, Pink nose, Gray horns, 4.2" tall, 4.75" long, not marked on bottom, Made in Japan, circa 1990s, **$6.00**

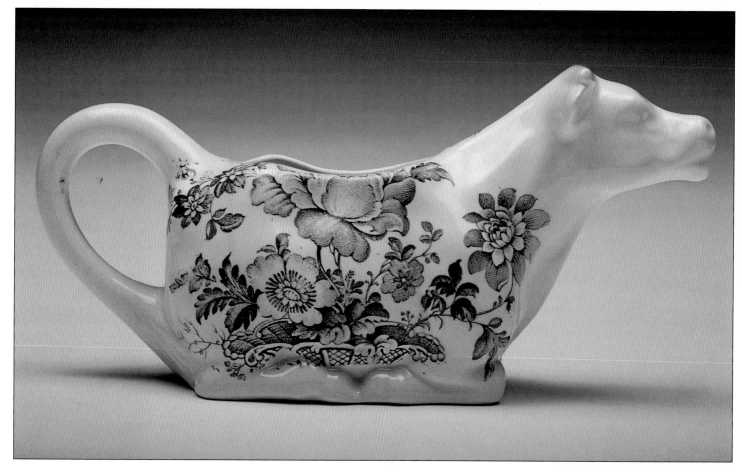

Cow, Brown and White, 3.5" tall, 7.25" long, laying down, marked on bottom in Brown: "Charlotte Royal Crownford Ironstone England", circa 1980s, **$26.00**

Cow, White with Blue wash, windmill scene, 4.5" tall, 6.75" wide, not marked on bottom, circa 1930s, **$35.00**

Cow, Gray, 4.5" tall, 6.75" long, not marked on bottom, circa 1950s, **$24.50**

Cow. **Left:** White with brown accents, 3.5" tall, 5" long, not marked on bottom, circa 1940s, **$6.50**
Right: White with Orange spots, 4.75" tall, 6.5" long, marked on bottom in Orange: "Made in Czecho-Slovakia", circa 1920s, **$26.00**

Cow. Left: Green, 4.75" tall, 4.5" long, not marked on bottom, circa 1950s, **$8.00**
Right: White with Dark Brown accents, 3.5" tall, 4" long, marked on bottom in Black: "Japan", circa 1950s, **$8.50**

Cow, Brown, 3.5" tall, 5.5" long, ribbon with metal bell around neck, not marked on bottom, circa 1960s, **$12.50**

Dog

Dogs descended from a wolf-like animal about 15 million years ago. It is thought that dogs and humans have been companions for about 14,000 years. The first dogs were used by people as guards, and later they were trained for herding livestock and assisting hunters for other animals for food. Today's dogs are still used to herd cattle and sheep on ranches, are loved as pets, and can be trained to assist police, rescue teams and handicapped people.

As mans best friend, dogs are prominent in any collection of figural pitchers. The prices for dog pitchers are driven up by customers who look for something different to add to their collections. Prices are more for any dog pitcher that is a specific breed, over one that looks like a mixed breed. It amazes us that we did not find more dog pitchers.

Dog, Green body, Red blaze, ears and tail, Yellow underside, 5" tall, 3" wide, marked on bottom in Red: "Germany", circa 1920s, **$45.00**

Dog, Man sitting in chair with a dog being the handle, Black, Brown and Green, 6" tall, 6.5" long, marked on bottom: Green mountain in wreath "Made in Japan Hand Painted', circa 1960s, **$19.50**

Dog, White with Black spots with Blue bone on nose, Red and Orange collar, 8.75" tall, 5.5" wide, marked on bottom: "Coco Dowley", Made in Japan, circa 1990s, **$9.50**

Dog, Black and White, 4.25" tall, 4.5" long
Left: marked on bottom in Black: "Ucagco China Made in Occupied Japan", circa 1945 to 1952, **$18.50**; **Right:** marked on bottom in Black: "Japan", circa late 1950s, **$12.50**

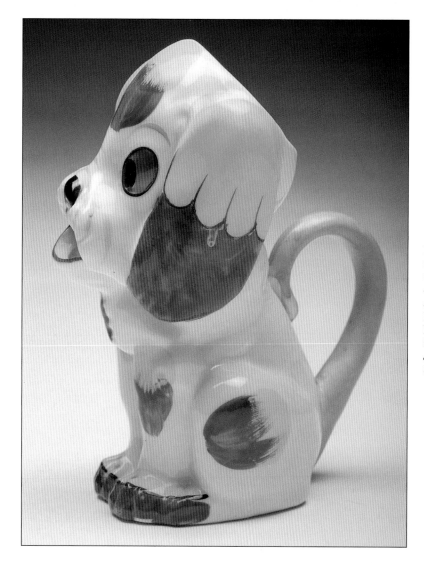

Dog, White with Yellow on top of ears and feet, Orange on bottom of ears and feet, Green and Yellow dots, Blue handle, 5.75" tall, 5" long, marked on bottom in Black: "Made in Japan", circa 1930s, **$28.50**

Dog, Collie, Brown, 4.25" tall, 5.5" long, marked on the bottom in Black: "UGC Made in Japan", circa 1950s, **$35.00**

Dog, Gray luster, Orange ears, Black and Blue eyes, Gold handle, 4" tall, 5" long, marked on bottom in Black: "Made in Japan", circa 1930s, **$16.50**

Dog, Wolfhound, White with Gold accents, miniature, 1.75" tall, 1.25" long, not marked on bottom, Made in Japan, circa 1950s, **$9.50**

Dog, White with Brown and Black accents, 6.75" tall, 5.5" long, marked on bottom: "Copyright", circa 1960s, **$12.50**

Dog, Scottie, White with Brown accents, Orange collar with Blue tag, 4.75" tall, 4.75" long, marked on bottom in Black: "Ucagco China Made in Occupied Japan", circa 1945 to 1952, **$35.00**

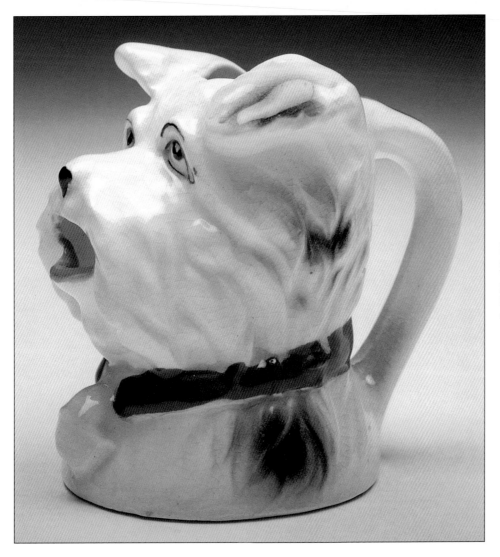

Dog, White with Black ears, Red collar and Yellow bell, 3.75" tall, 4" long, not marked on bottom, Made in Japan, circa 1950s, **$24.00**

Dog, Dachshund, Brown, 4.1" tall, 3.25" wide, not marked on the bottom, circa 1960s, **$24.50**

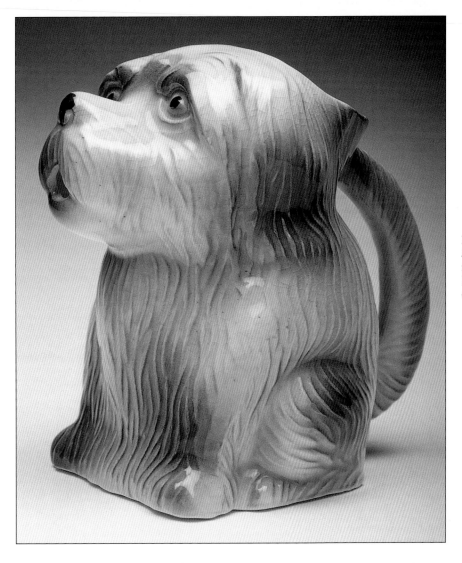

Dog, White with Black, 5.75" tall, 6" long, marked on bottom in Black: "Made in Japan", circa 1960s, **$18.50**

Dog. **Left:** White, 3" tall, 3.25" long, marked on bottom with Black and Gold foil label: "HIC Japan", circa 1990s, **$7.50**
Right: Hound, White with Brown, 2.75" tall, 2.5" long, incised on side: "Japan", marked on bottom in Black: "Made in Japan", circa 1930s, **$14.50**

Dog. **Left:** White with Green accents with pink bow, 3" tall, 3" long, marked on bottom in Black: "C762", circa 1950s, **$8.50**
Right: White with Black accents, 4" tall, 5.25" long, marked on bottom in Black: "Made in Japan", circa 1950s, **$19.50**

Dog, White with Orange and Green accents, 5" tall, 4.25" long, marked on bottom in Black: "Hand painted TT Made in Japan", circa 1930s, **$24.50**

Duck

Ducks are part of the bird family but are distinct with water repellent feathers along with webbed feet for moving through the water. They live in all parts of the world except Antarctica. Many species of ducks who generally live in one area migrate to a warmer area to raise their young. Their annual migrations can be thousands of miles in distance.

Ducks are a source of meat and feathers. There are eight distinct groups of ducks, of which five live in North America. Favorites include the Mallard, Muscovy, Pekin, Pintail and Wood Duck. Most of the domestic ducks originated from wild Mallards.

Fowl of all kinds fit well with a kitchen theme. There are many types of duck pitchers that can be found with diligent looking.

Duckling, Popping out of egg, White with iridized finish, Pink and Purple flowers, 6.75" tall, 7" long, not marked on bottom, Made in Korea, circa 1990s, $**8.50**

115

Duck, White, 4.6" tall, 4" long, marked on bottom: "Japan", circa 1990s, **$6.00**

Opposite Page:
Duck, Blue coat, Pink hat, Brown bill and handle, 4.4" tall, 7" long, not marked on bottom, Made by Spaulding China, circa 1940s and 1950s, **$35.00**

Duck, Mallard, Green head, Brown and Green body, cat tail handle, 16.25" tall, 7.5" long, Majolica style, marked on bottom in Black: "St. Clement Made in France", also embossed with "KG SC 375", circa 1950s, **$145.00**

Duck, Mallard, Green head, Brown and Green body, cattail handle, 12.5" tall, 6" long, Majolica style, marked on bottom: "SC France", circa 1950s, **$95.00**

Duck, Mallard, Green head, Brown and Green body, cat tail handle, 6.6" tall, 6" long, Midwest Pottery, not marked on bottom, circa 1940s, **$35.00**

Duck, White, 9.5"
tall, 9" long, not
marked on bottom,
circa 1990s, **$9.50**

Duck, White with Blue bow around neck, yellow bill and feet, 7.5" tall, 7" long, not marked on bottom, circa 1990s, **$12.50**

Duck. Left: White with Red accents, 2.25" tall, 2" long, not marked on bottom, circa 1950s, **$6.50**
Right: White, 3.5" tall, 3.25" long, not marked on bottom, circa 1990s, **$5.00**

Duck, Miniature, 1.5" tall, 1.5" long, not marked on bottom, Made in Japan, circa 1950s, **$9.50 each**
Left: Green
Center: Blue
Right: Gold

Duck, White with Brown accents, Yellow bill, 2.75" tall, 5" long, not marked on bottom, circa 1940s, **$6.50**

Duck, Black with Gold accents, 3" tall, 7.5" long, not marked on bottom, Made in Japan, circa 1950s, **$9.50**

Duck, Mallard, Gray with Brown, 3.5" tall, 5" long, marked on
bottom: "© Otagiri 1981", Made in Japan, **$7.50**

Duck, White with Yellow bill and Yellow, Green and Blue wings, 8" tall, 5.5" long, not marked on bottom, California pottery, **$24.50**

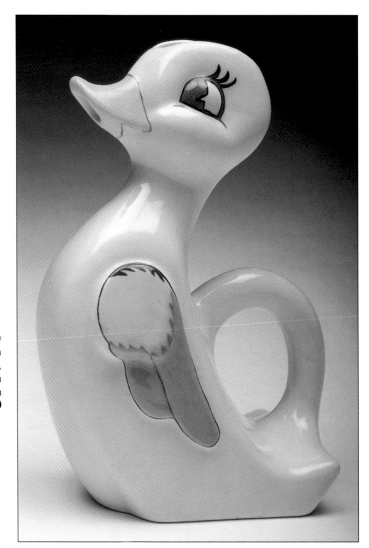

Elephant

The largest mammal to live on land is the elephant, and it is second to the giraffe for being the tallest. There are two types of elephants: the African elephant that lives in the Sahara area of Africa and has large ears and the Asian elephant that lives in the southeastern part of Asia and India with small ears.

The most famous elephant of all was named Jumbo, the largest in captivity weighing 14,000 pounds and being 11 feet tall. Jumbo was at the London Zoo for 17 years before being brought to America in 1882 by P. T. Barnum for his circus show. Jumbo is attributed with inspiring widespread interest in elephants.

Elephants have often been a favorite subject for designers of creamers and pitchers. Collectors have helped to drive up the prices on these pieces. Folklore has it that if an elephant is found with its trunk up, that means good luck. We have found many made with the less expensive ceramics and thin trunks, causing many of them to be damaged.

Elephant, Dumbo, Gray, 5.5" tall, 5.75" long, marked on bottom: "© Disney Mexico", circa 1990s, **$28.00**

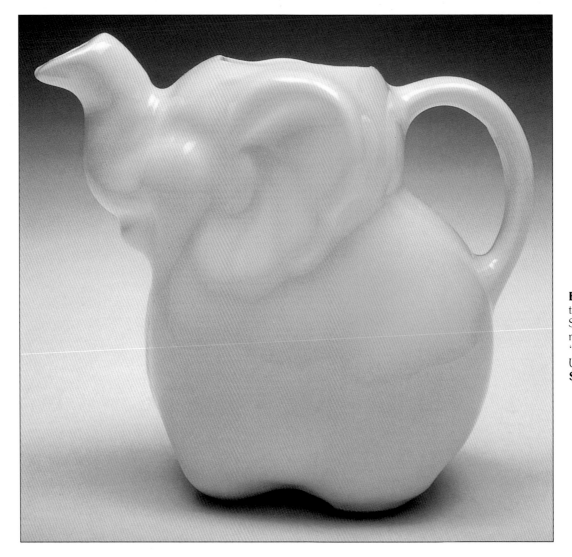

Elephant, Yellow, 4.5" tall, 5" long, old Shawnee mould, marked on bottom: "McCoy", Made in U.S.A., circa 2004, **$18.00**

Elephant, White, 4.5" tall, 4.75" long, not marked on bottom, Made in Japan, circa 1990s, **$7.50**

Elephant, Gray with Brown, Green and Yellow plaid blanket on back, Brown handle, 3.6" tall, 4" long, marked on bottom in Green: Mountain peak, wreath, "Made in Japan hand painted", circa 1970s, **$9.50**

Elephant, Green, Black accents on feet, White handle with Black accents, 4.75" tall, 5" long, marked on bottom: wide crown over "WG ™", M, Germany, Made by Goebel", circa 1935 to 1950, **$45.00**

Elephant, Gray, Purple headdress and blanket, Purple handle, 4" tall, 6.25" long, marked with Gold decal on bottom: "Giftcraft Taiwan", circa 1990s, **$8.00**

Elephant, Bluish Gray with Pink ears and tip of trunk, Orange belt, 4.4" tall, 4" long, marked on bottom in Red: "Made in Germany", circa 1930s, **$35.00**

Elephant, 4.5" tall, 5.25" long, marked on bottom: "Patented U.S.A", Made by Shawnee Pottery, circa 1940s and 1950s
Left: White with Red inside of ears, Brown accents on hooves, $**38.00**
Right: White with flower decals, Red outside of ears, Gold on handle and tip of trunk, **$95.00**

Elephant, Orange with Yellow trunk handle and ears, 7" tall, 6.5" long, marked on bottom in Black: "Made in Japan", circa 1960s, **$10.00**

Elephant. Left: White, Gray ears, 2.25" tall, 2.25" long, not marked on bottom, circa 1950s, **$7.50**
Right: Brown, 2.75" tall, 3" long, not marked on bottom, circa 1950s, **$9.50**

Elephant, White with Pink ears, Black accents on feet, 4.75" tall, 5" long, marked on bottom in Black: "Ucagco China Made in Occupied Japan", circa 1945 to 1952, **$28.00**

Elephant. **Left:** White with Blue flowers, 3.75" tall, 4.5" long, marked on bottom in Brown: "mh '51", Shawnee copy cat, **$16.00**
Right: Blue with White flowers, 4" tall, 6" long, marked on bottom with Gold and Black label: "Josef Originals Korea", circa 1990s, **$14.50**

Elephant. **Left:** White, 4.5" tall, 4" long, not marked on bottom, circa 1990s, **$6.00**;
Right: White with Yellow, Blue and Pink accents, 5" tall, 5" long, not marked on
bottom, Made by American Bisque, circa 1940s and 1950s, **$28.00**

Elephant. **Left:** White with Brown speckles, 5.75" tall, 5.25" long, not marked on bottom, circa 1980s, **$8.50** **Right:** Blue, 5.25" tall, 5" long, marked on bottom in Black: "Made in Japan", circa 1990s, **$7.50**

Elephant, White, 4" tall, 7.75" long, not marked on bottom, circa 1970s, **$9.50**

Elephant, Gray with a Green coat and Yellow pants, Orange vest, 5.75" tall, 5.25" long, incised on the side with the number: "6641-1", not marked on bottom, Made in Germany, circa 1930s, **$45.00**

Elephant, Made by American Bisque, circa 1940s and 1950s
Left: White with Blue ears, 5" tall, 5" long, not marked on bottom, **$18.50**;
Right: White with Yellow ears, 4.5" tall, 3.5" long, not marked on bottom, **$12.50**

Elephant, **Left:** Gray with Pink ears, Blue collar with Yellow bell, 5" tall, 4.5" long, not marked on bottom, Made in Japan, circa 1960s, **$14.50** **Right:** Beige, 6" tall, 5" long, marked on bottom in Black: "Japan", circa 1960s, **$14.50**

Elephant, Pink with Gray accents, 6" tall, 4" long, marked on bottom in Black: 'Stewart B. McCullock", Made in California, circa 1940s, **$24.00**

Fish

Fish have been on the earth for over 500 million years, living first on the bottom of the seas and were covered with heavy scales. The modern fish came from the Mesozoic times 250 million years ago. Different fish live all over the world in fresh and salt water. Used primarily as a food source, they can be raised in tanks at home as a pet.

Fish pitchers are elusive for a collector to locate, perhaps because their shape is not conducive to making a figural pitcher.

Fish, Miniature, Blue, 2.5" tall, 1.5" long, not marked on bottom, circa 1940s, **$9.50**

Fish, Yellow sponge ware luster, Orange bubbles and accents on fins, White handle, 4.5" tall, 4" long, marked on the bottom in Black: "Made in Japan", circa 1950s, **$45.00**

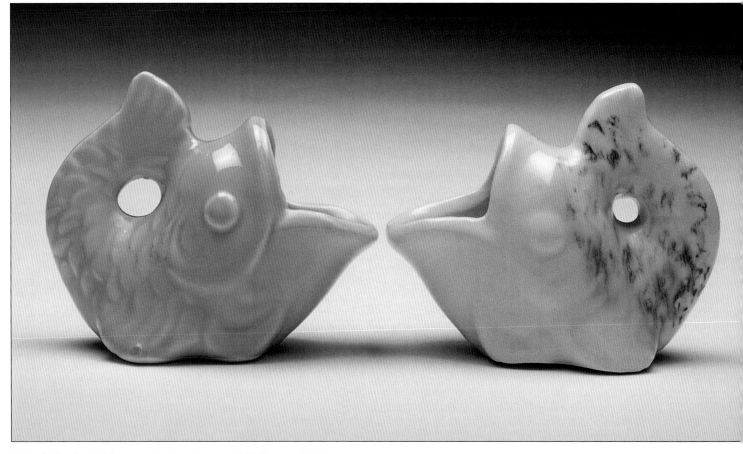

Fish, 3.5" tall, 4.5" long, marked on bottom: "USA", circa 1940s
Left: Turquoise, **$8.50**
Right: White with drip glaze, **$7.50**

Fish, Gold, 3.25" tall, 5.5" long, not marked on bottom, circa 1980s, **$9.50**

Fish, Green and Brown, 3.4" tall, 5.5" long, not marked on bottom, circa 1970s, $**12.50**

Fox

The fox is a member of the dog family. With a sharp nose and a bushy tail, foxes can be found worldwide with the exception of Antarctica and southeast Asia. They generally live in wooded areas and some deserts. As a skilled hunter, foxes quickly catch their prey. This skill also enables them to avoid capture, causing them to be sporting prey and therefore a nuisance to farmers. The royal British passion for fox hunts grew from practical causes. The fox is about 25" long with the tail adding an additional 15" in length. They weigh 10 pounds, on the average.

What a wonderful and exciting animal to feature as a creamer or pitcher. But, these foxes, too, are an elusive item to the collector.

Fox, Brown with Green leaves and Purple grapes, 4.25" tall, 4" long, marked on bottom: "Fitz and Floyd 1991", **$15.00**

Frog

During the Jurassic period, 213 million years ago, frogs made their appearance on earth. As amphibians, they are cold-blooded animals. They spend part of their lives in the water and part on land. A frog can be found on every continent except Antarctica. The unusually large hind legs of the frog enable them to travel great distances. Their long tongues enable them to reach far for their prey.

Artists who choose subject matter for pitchers must not have liked frogs a lot, since there don't seem to be many around. Frogs can be appropriate as a bathroom adornment as well as a kitchen one.

Frog, Grayish Green and Beige, Beige spots, 5" tall, 5.5" long, not marked on bottom, Made in Japan, circa 1980s, **$12.50**

Frog, White and Gray, Brown twig handle, 3.25" tall, 4.5" long, marked on bottom in Black: "Fitz and Floyd, Inc. © MCMLXXVII FF, 1977", **$18.50**

Frog, Green, 3.25" tall, 5.25" long, marked on bottom in Gold foil label: "VG Japan", circa 1970s, **$9.50**

Frog, Green with Green spots, Pink bow, 4.5" tall, 4.5" long, miniature frog sitting on the top of the frog's head, not marked on bottom, circa 1990s, **$12.50**

Giraffe

The giraffe is the tallest animal; it can reach a height of 18 feet. Their homeland is in Africa, south of the Sahara Desert and their favorite food is tender leaves of high trees, fruit and berries. If needed, the giraffe can survive several weeks without drinking water.

Giraffes have a unique spotted brown pattern over their bodies with a yellow background and white outline surrounding each patch. Each giraffe has its own distinct pattern, not unlike a human fingerprint.

To our delight, we found a giraffe creamer to include in this book. Normally, the giraffe is not the right shape for a pitcher, with its long neck, but in this case only the head was used, perhaps the only way it might have been designed.

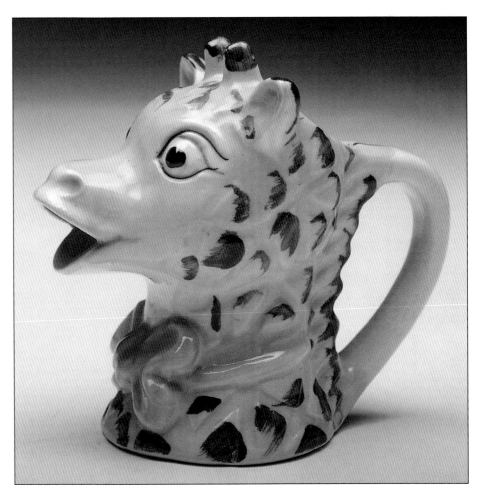

Giraffe, head, Yellow with Brown accents, Pink bow, 4" tall, 4.5" long, marked on bottom in Black: "Hand painted Made in Japan", circa 1950s, **$28.50**

Goat

In Biblical times, a goat was a common animal used as a source for milk and meat, and sometimes for a sacrifice. They are believed to have been raised around men for about 9,000 years. While their milk is similar to cow's milk, it is easier to digest and makes a good choice for babies and elderly people. Goat cheese is quite creamy, comes in many varieties, and is used in many gourmet foods. A goat's furry coat can be shorn and used to weave clothing. The types of goat's wool include Angora, Cashmere, and Mohair.

While goats are usually thought of as livestock, they also make wonderful pets. Pygmy goats, especially, are suited for this use, since they are small in size. Goats are amazingly friendly and are curious to find out what is going on.

The goat is not often found as the subject for a pitcher, a fact we found hard to believe and hope more show up.

Goat, Mountain, Yellow with Gray horns, 4.25" tall, 5.25" long, Orange interior, marked on bottom in Black: "MW Co. hand painted Made in Germany", circa 1920s, **$48.00**

Horse

Throughout history, horses have served man's many needs by being a mode of transportation and assistance in getting work done. Early hunters utilized horses to chase down other animals for food. Horses were used to plow the fields of pioneers and even today's cowboy uses a horse to roundup livestock. Horses are also seen running a race, in a parade, at the rodeo or on pleasure rides.

An unusual aspect of the horse is the type of measurement used to see how tall it is. Horses are measured in "hands," from the top of the withers to the ground. A hand is 4 inches, which is the average width of an adult hand. An average horse is 15 hands, or 60 inches tall.

Horse items have long been favorite collectibles, although we have found only a couple of horse pitchers. Because of the strong collector base for horses, you will have to pay a little more to get a horse creamer.

Horse, Brown with Black mane, White handle, 4.5" tall, 5.75" long, marked on the bottom in Black: "UCG Made in Japan", circa 1960s, **$38.00**

Horse, Carousel, White with Black mane, Blue and Black beaded collar, 4" tall, 4.5" long, marked on bottom in Black: "Hand painted, Made in Japan", circa 1950s, **$24.50**

Horse, Yellow with Green drip glaze accents, 4.25" tall, 4.5" long, not marked on bottom, circa 1960s, **$12.50**

Koala

A common misconception about the Koala is that they are a member of the bear family, which they definitely are not. The Koala is a type of marsupial, meaning they give birth to immature young, closely related to the Wombat. Their undeveloped young travel to a pouch where it grows until it is developed. The Koala is found in Australia, New Guinea and surrounding islands. A definition for Koala means doesn't drink and originates from the Aborigine language. The Koala feeds on the tender leaves and branches of the eucalyptus tree and receives all the liquid it needs from this food source. They rarely are seen drinking any water.

Finding a Koala creamer was a real treat, but also a surprise. We can only assume that possibly it was a souvenir from Australia.

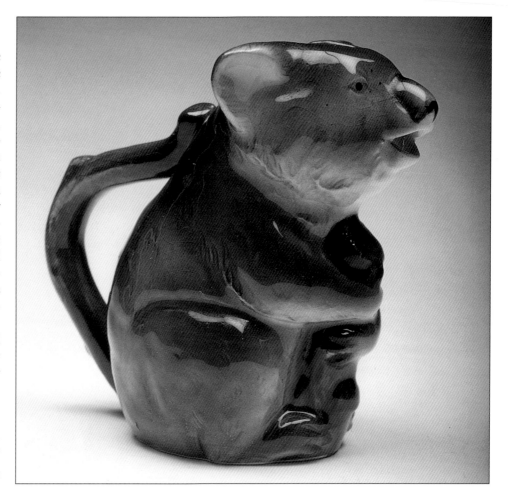

Koala, Brown, 4.5" tall, 4.5" long, marked on bottom in Black: "Japan", circa 1960s, **$38.00**

Lion

The lion has long been known as the king of beasts. It is the largest member of the cat family and almost everyone envisions Africa with a majestic, roaring lion as part of the scenery. Their favorite foods are antelope, gazelle, deer and zebra. Lions live in a pride, consisting of a dominate male and several females with young. The females do most of the hunting. Lions often can be seen in zoos and circuses.

A folklore tale, *The Lion and the Mouse*, relates that these two became friends and helped each other. The Disney Studios movie *Lion King* exposed many children to lions for the first time.

It was unusual to find a lion used as a cream pitcher. Being dressed up in human form makes us think this one must be a character from a story. Hopefully other examples of lion pitchers will turn up.

Lion, Brown, Black monocle, Black and Gold bow tie, 5.25" tall, 4.75" long, marked on bottom in Black: "MW Co. hand painted Made in Germany", circa 1930s, **$48.00**

Moose

Moose can be found in forests around the world. The biggest variety is one from Alaska that weighs 1800 pounds. Moose are the largest member of the deer family and their favorite food is tender shrubs and underwater plants. The male moose, called a bull, has a massive antler structure that is shaped like a hand. The antlers can have a spread of six feet and weigh 85 pounds. While a wolf or bear can easily kill a young moose, once fullgrown they become a formidable adversary. Moose are shy and timid, even though they are massive looking. Bullwinkle was a favorite moose cartoon character on Saturday morning television.

As a creamer, the moose doesn't seem to be a popular choice for designers since only a few have been found. We suspect that the delicate detail of their antlers makes a moose hard to replicate.

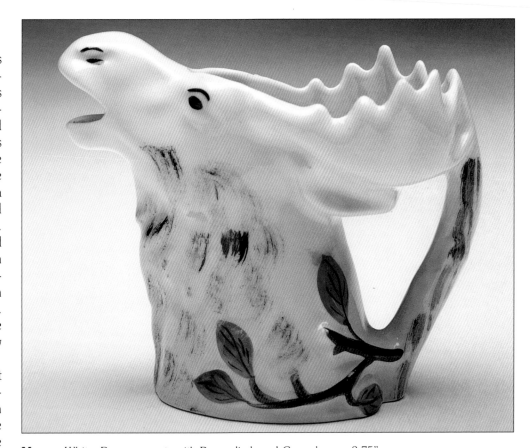

Moose, White, Brown accents with Brown limb and Green leaves, 3.75" tall, 4.5" long, marked on bottom: "Clinchfield Artware Pottery Hand Painted Erwin Tennessee", circa 1940s, **$60.00**

Moose, Brown with shaded White bottom, 3.5" tall, 5.25" long, marked on bottom in Red: "Made in Czecho-Slovakia", circa 1920s, **$65.00**

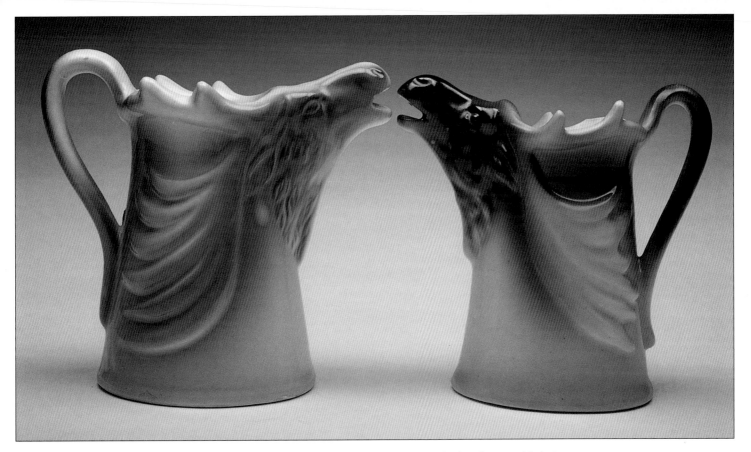

Moose. **Left:** Brown with Blue base, 5" tall, 5" long, reproduction of old one, not marked on bottom, Made in China, circa 2000, **$15.00**

Right: Brown with Blue base, 4.75" tall, 4.75" long, marked on bottom in Red: "Made in Czecho-Slovakia", circa 1930s, **$48.00**

Moose, Beige with Brown, 5"
tall, 6" long, not marked on
bottom, Made in Japan, circa
1990s, **$8.50**

Mouse

In an ancient language from Asia, the word "mouse" is defined as a thief. What an appropriate name this is, since mice live in houses and barns and steal food. Their sharp teeth enable them to eat grains and gnaw through cardboard. Mice live all over the world, near humans, so that they can eat the remains of human food. In the wild, owls, hawks, snakes, coyotes, and house cats all like to eat mice

For research purposes, mice have proven to be valuable for research scientists learning about diseases and the affects of drugs. People also keep certain types of mice as pets.

A famous mouse that everyone recognizes is Walt Disney's cartoon character, Mickey Mouse. Also, the cartoon duo of Tom and Jerry features a cat and a mouse in a variety of interesting situations. We found only a couple of mice creamers.

Mouse, White with Green accents on dress, 4.75" tall, 3.75" wide, not marked on bottom, circa 1990s, **$9.50**

Mouse, Brown with Pink dress holding a gray watering can, 4.5" tall, 5.5" long, marked on the bottom with a paper label: "Applause Inc. Woodland Hills, Ca 91365-4183 © Applause Inc Made in Taiwan ROC", circa 1990s, **$9.50**

Owl

The owl is classified as a bird of prey because they hunt and kill their food. Living alone in tall trees, owls hunt at nighttime. Their keen eyesight and high speed enable them to rapidly catch their prey. A flow of air over their wings enables their flight to be almost silent. The "wise old" owl is a native to many forests around the United States and over 200 different species of owls live around the world. Owls are of tremendous benefit to man by feeding on rodents that are harmful to crops.

In ancient Greek mythology, owls were sacred to Athena, the goddess of wisdom. This is probably where the term "wise as an owl" comes from. A classic children's poem, *The Owl and the Pussycat*, written by Edward Lear in 1871, tells of an unusual love between an owl and a cat.

This is another type of animal that doesn't seem to be used much as a creamer. However, they make a fun addition to any collection.

Owl, White with Brown accents around face and near feet, 5.5" tall, 4.5" long, not marked on bottom, Made in Japan, circa 1980s, **$12.50**

Owl, Gray, Red eyes and beak, 4" tall, 4.25" long, marked on bottom in Blue: "Royal Bayreuth Bavaria", circa 1930s, **$175.00**

Owl, White with Blue floral, 4.5" tall, 4.25" long, marked on bottom in Blue: "Made in China", circa 1990s, **$7.50**

Owl, Brown, 2.25" tall, 2.75" long, not marked on bottom, circa 1980s, **$6.50**

Owl, White with Gray and Orange accents, 3" tall, 4" long, marked on bottom in Black: "Fitz and Floyd, Inc. © MCMLXXVII FF", circa 1970s, **$17.50**

Owl, Gray with Orange and Black accents, 7.25" tall, 5" long, marked on bottom in Black: "Italy", circa 1970s, **$24.00**

Penguin

Penguins are a type of bird unable to fly. Their wings, however, are used to propel them underwater at amazingly fast speeds. All penguins in the wild are found south of the equator in cold ocean waters. Their thick feathers form a waterproof layer of air that insulates them. They also have a thick layer of fat to keep them warm. The 17 different species of penguins are at home near the Galapagos Islands, New Zealand, Australia, the coast of South America, southern Africa and Antarctica. They consume crabs, fish, shrimp and squid.

For centuries, penguins have lived solitary lives away from humans and other animals. They are easily disturbed by human activities such as fishing and contaminants in the water. A conservation effort is being made to protect them and many zoos have penguin displays to educate the public.

The penguin is an elusive pitcher to find.

Penguin, Black and White with Red and Green plaid hat, 6" tall, 3.5" wide, not marked on bottom, circa 1980s, **$14.50**

Pheasant

A native of China, the pheasant has long been a favorite bird of hunters. Their beautiful plumage was formerly used to decorate ladies' hats in large numbers, and in the making of fishing flies. While there are over 35 species of pheasants, the Ring Necked pheasant is the most recognized. Pheasant cocks have brightly colored feathers while pheasant hens have only subdued coloring. Though they can fly short distances, pheasants spends most of their time on the ground in search of favorite bugs, seeds and roots.

The beautiful plumage on the pheasant makes it a very attractive pitcher. We were pleased to find a couple of examples.

Pheasant, Beige and Brown, Green head, 3.75" tall, 6.5" long, marked on bottom: "© Otagiri 1984 Japan", **$8.50**

Pheasant, Green head, Orange and Black body, White handle, 10.5" tall, 11.5" long, marked on bottom in Black: "Made in Italy", circa 1980s, **$24.00**

Pig

From the family *Suidae*, pigs were among the animals roaming the earth over 6 million years ago. During the stone age, they were domesticated as a food source and their fat (lard) was used as in cooking and making soap. Pigs have poor eyesight, but their keen smell enables them to find food, even when buried in the ground. They have no sweat glands in their thick hide and therefore they roll in mud to keep cool during hot months. Over one billion pigs are raised yearly around the world, and China raises half of them. The pigs are one of the easiest animals to train, so they were one of the earliest animals used in circus acts. *The Three Little Pigs* story has been read to many adoring young children.

We have been amazed to see so many pig pitchers. People seem to love them as a kitchen motif.

Pig, Green, 4.5" tall, 5" long, old American Bisque mould, marked on bottom: "McCoy", circa 2004, **$15.00**

Pig, "Smiley" , Cream with Pink flower and Green leaves, 4.5" tall, 4.75" long, marked on bottom: "Patented Smiley U.S.A.", Made by Shawnee Pottery, circa 1940s and 1950s, **$45.00**

Pig, Beige with Black nose, eyes and feet, 4.25" tall, 5" long, marked on bottom: "A Country Critter by Mary", circa 1980s, **$8.50**

180

Pig, White, Brown ears, Hand painted Green tuxedo accents, 4" tall, 4" long, marked on bottom: "Made in Japan", circa 1950s, **$12.50**

Opposite Page:
Pig, White with Green tic tac toe design and Brown accents, 3.75" tall, 5.5" long, paper label says: "Made in California, Rio Hondo Potteries, El Monte California", circa 1940s and 1950s, **$14.00**

Pig, White with hand painted Pink and Brown flowers, 3.5" tall, 3.5" long, not marked on bottom, Made in California, circa 1940s, **$9.50**

Pig, White with multi colored spots, Orange bow, 8" tall, 9" long, Made by American Bisque, not marked on bottom, circa 1940s and 1950s, **$85.00**

Pig, Green hat, Gray coat, White apron, Orange handle, 3" tall, 2.25" long, marked on the bottom in Red: "Japan', circa 1920s, **$19.50**

Pig, Pink, Blue hat and bow on tail, 4.5" tall, 6" long, marked on bottom: "Pat. Pending", Made by Spaulding China, Royal Copley line, circa 1940s and 1950s, **$35.00**

Pig, Blue and Pink, 6" tall, 5.25" long, not marked on bottom, circa 1940s and 1950s, **$25.00**

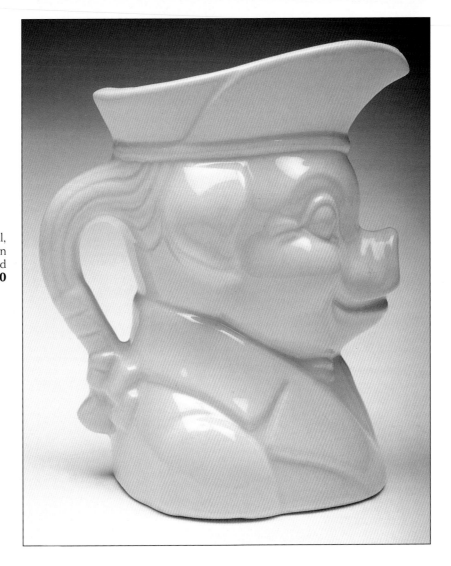

Pig, Beige, 9" tall, 7.5" long, marked on bottom in Black: "Porky Pitcher Fitz and Floyd, Inc. © MCMLXXVII FF", circa 1977, **$24.50**

Pig, White, 5.75" tall, 5" wide, dressed in colonial outfit, not marked on bottom, circa 1950s, **$16.00**

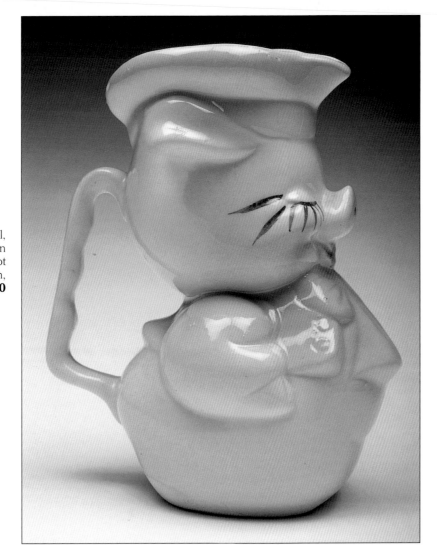

Pig, Pink, 3.5" tall, 2.75" long, not marked on bottom, Made in Germany, circa 1950s, **$24.50**

Pig, Blue with brown accents, miniature, 1" tall, 2.25" long, not marked on bottom, circa 1960s, **$6.00**

Pig, White with Orange accents, 5" tall, 5.5" long, not marked on bottom, Made by American Bisque, circa 1950s and 1960s, **$18.00**

Pig. Left: White, 3.25" tall, 5.5" long, not marked on bottom, circa 1990s, **$7.50**
Right: Pink, 3.75" tall, 5.5" long, not marked on bottom, circa 1980s, **$7.50**

Pig. Left: White with Brown speckles, 5" tall, 6" long, not marked on bottom, circa 1980s, **$9.50**
Right: White with Black accents, 4.6" tall, 5.25" long, not marked on bottom, circa 1970s, **$8.50**

Pig. Left: White, 3.75" tall, 6" long, not marked on bottom, circa 1980s, **$8.50**; **Right:** White with Yellow and Orange flowers, 3" tall, 5.5" long, marked on bottom with Red and Gold foil label: "Original Lenwile Ardalt Artware Japan", circa 1980s, **$9.50**

Rhinoceros

The rhinoceros is a large land mammal with five species from Asia and Africa. The largest rinoceros is the White Rhino from Africa. It can get up to six feet tall and weigh close to 3.5 tons. They have thick skin on a solid muscular body. Their short legs enable them to run quickly, even with the weight they carry. They consume grass, branches and shrubs. At the end of their nose, rhinoseroses have a horn that has the fiber of human fingernails and continues to grow throughout the life of the rhino. In certain cultures, the horn is considered to have special healing powers. For this reason, it is hunted for the horn only. This senseless killing has caused several treaties to be written to protect the rhino. Many rhinos have been captured and placed in African preserves so they can be better protected from illegal poachers.

It was fortunate to find a rhinoceros pitcher to include here.

Rhinoceros, Gray, Orange accents, has on a coat and holding a nap sack, 4.4" tall, 4.5" long, marked on the bottom in Red: "Made in Germany", circa 1930s, **$48.00**

Sheep

For thousands of years, people have kept sheep as a food source and for their wool to make clothing. Surprisingly, China is the biggest producer of sheep today, followed by Australia. Around the world, there are over 800 breeds of sheep.

A baby lamb, an immature sheep, is a common sight in Spring, frolicking around in a field, that proclaims a new growth season. Sheep have been used as decorations associated with the Christian Easter season.

Sheep creamers have not yielded many examples.

Sheep, Lamb, White, flower transfer decal on front and back legs, Pink accents on ears and nose, Red and Gold bow, 4.5" tall, 4" long, not marked on bottom, Made by American Bisque, circa 1940s and 1950s, **$35.00**

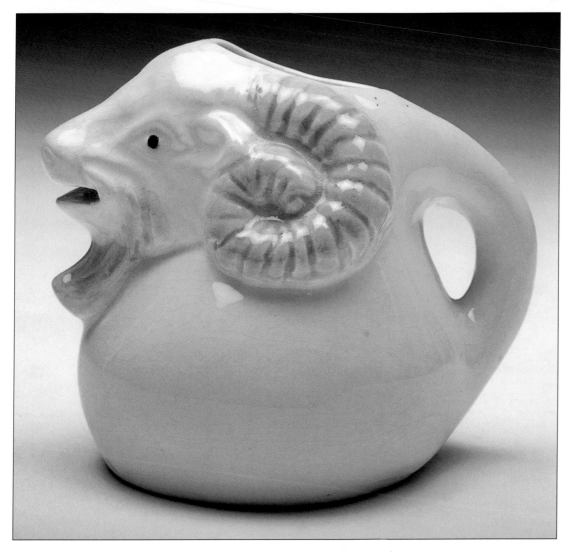

Sheep, Mountain, Yellow with Brown horns, 4" tall, 5" long, marked on bottom in Brown: "Mexico", circa 1980s, **$12.00**

Sheep, Beige,
Orange collar and
bells around neck,
4" tall, 4.75" long,
marked on bottom:
'Otagiri 1983
Japan", **$7.50**

Sheep, White with Green and Gold flowers, 4.75" tall, 7.5" long, marked on bottom in Black: "Genuine Staffordshire Hand painted Shorter & Sons, Ltd England", circa 1960s, **$45.00**

Sheep, White with Blue, Yellow bow, 3.5" tall, 4" long, marked on bottom in Black: "Hand painted, Made in Japan", circa 1950s, **$28.00**

Squirrel

The squirrel is in the family of rodents. Their sharp teeth and strong jaws enable them to chew through nuts, roots, seeds and cones. Their long legs and sharp claws assist them as they jump among branches and their tail help glide them through the air. The tail also serves to signal the presence of a predator or something unfamiliar as it shakes and they chatter loudly. Their nest is of great importance to them for it provides a secure home, a place to raise their young, and a place to store their food.

We felt lucky to find this charming squirrel pitcher to include.

Squirrel, Brown and White, 3" tall, 5.25" long, marked on bottom in Black: "© 1972 ENESCO Japan", **$9.50**

Turkey

Turkeys are birds related to chickens and pheasants. American Indians domesticated the turkey around 1000AD. Beautiful wild turkey feathers adorned many of their clothes and tools. A wild turkey weighs around 15 pounds and can fly great lengths. Found in wooded areas, it consumes fruits, grains, insects and nuts. At night, the wild turkey roosts in trees, away from any predators. The domestic turkey can weigh up to 50 pounds, so because of this extra weight, it cannot fly.

As a creamer, this is another hard pitcher to find.

Turkey, Brown with Red head and Black accents, 3.5" tall, 5.25" long, not marked on bottom, circa 1980s, **$9.50**

Turtle

Over 250 different types of turtles are known around the world and 50 types are found in the United States and Canada. Turtles date back 185 million years and are the only reptile to have a shell, which serves as a protective covering in times of distress. The leather-back turtle is the largest, known to grow up to eight feet in length. The smallest turtle is the bog turtle, only four inches long. The famous fairy tale, *The Tortoise and the Hare* has delighted many children.

It is hard to find a turtle-shaped pitcher.

Turtle, Green with Orange, Black and Yellow shell, 2.25" tall, 4" long, marked on the bottom in Red: "Japan", circa 1930s, **$45.00**
Note: This is a good copy of a Royal Bayreuth turtle creamer

Water Buffalo

The water buffalo is a type of wild oxen. Farmers have utilized them to plow fields for thousands of years. The water buffalo of India is the largest known variety, being 6.5" feet tall with horns that can measure up to 12 feet wide.

They spend much of their day in the water, which makes them ideal for rice farming. They easily plow through mud. A smaller water buffalo lives in the Philippine Islands and is used there in farming also.

In certain cultures, water buffalo are a source for milk for their owners. It was a surprise to find one to include here.

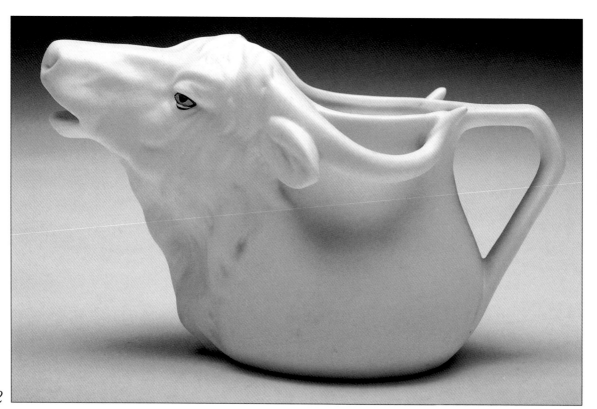

Water Buffalo, White, 4.25" tall, 4.5" long, not marked on bottom, circa 1930s, **$24.50**

Whale

Whales are the largest animals on earth. The Blue Whale is the largest type, weighing over 150 tons and being up to 35 yards long. The smallest whale is the Beluga, at only 5 yards long. Whales live in groups called "pods." A whale calf, or baby whale, usually stays with its mother about a year, but there are a couple of types in which the baby can stay with its mother up to three years. Whales communicate with each other by a variety of sounds, some of which a human can not hear. Humpback whales make the most distinctive sounds, as though they are singing. Cold water areas of the Arctic and Antarctic have an abundant supply of plankton on which whales feed. After the water starts to freeze, whales make long migrations to give birth and raise their young in warmer water.

We were surprised to find a whale as a creamer. This one was located, of course, at a gift shop on the beach. It is unusual, and, like others, probably was made as a souvenir.

Whale, Gray and Blue, 3.5" tall, 5.75" long, not marked on bottom, circa 1980s, **$19.50**

Wolf

Wolves belong to the dog family, *Canidae*, and are the largest members. Their eerie howl is a distinctive sound in nature. Wolves have been portrayed in literature and movies as villains, when they are really skillful hunters. They naturally feed on deer, elk, moose and caribou. As man invades their territory, they are forced to kill livestock. They live in family groups known as "packs." Within each pack, one male dominates over the rest in a social order. Wolves became known to many children as part of the fairy tale, *Little Red Riding Hood*.

A creamer listed in this chapter actually represents two animals, the wolf and a swan. We thought this combination was unusual. Since it is from Czechoslovakia, we assume it represents a fairytale or folklore from that region but have been unable to uncover the significance of these animals together.

Wolf spout, Brown, White swan handle with Green base, 3.6" tall, 5.25" long, marked on bottom in Red: "Made in Czecho-Slovakia 31", circa early 1930s, **$125.00**

Yak

The Yak is another type of wild oxen at home in Tibet, which has a very cold region. A long, heavy coat provides the Yak with protection against severe weather. It weighs 1200 pounds and stands over 6 feet tall at maturity. Even though the Yak is quite large, it is very agile and able to travel over snow-covered hills and rocky areas, plus be able to swim in rivers. The local residents completely utilize the Yak for food and the transportation of people and mail. A yak's hide is used as leather for boots and saddles. The long hair is woven into cloth.

Since a yak is another milk producer, it might be natural to find one as a creamer. For us, it was surprising enough to find it as a pitcher.

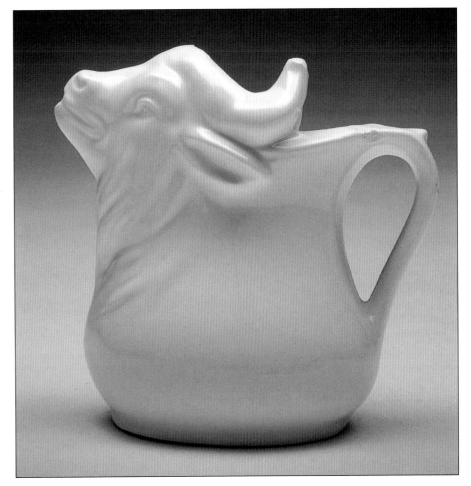

Yak, White, 3.5" tall, 6" long, not marked on bottom, circa 1980s, **$9.50**

Bibliography

Books

Barta, Dale & Diane and Helen M. Rose. *Czechoslovakian Glass & Collectibles.* Paducah, Kentucky: Collector Books, 1992.

Chipman, Jack. *Collector's Encyclopedia of California Pottery.* Paducah, Kentucky: Collector Books, 1999.

Devine, Joe and Leslie & Marjorie Wolfe. *Collector's Guide to Royal Copley Book 1.* Paducah, Kentucky: Collector Books, 1999.

Devine, Joe and Leslie & Marjorie Wolfe. *Collector's Guide to Royal Copley Book 2.* Paducah, Kentucky: Collector Books, 1999.

Forsythe, Ruth A. *Made in Czechoslovakia.* Marietta, Ohio: Richardson Printing Corp., 1982.

Forsythe, Ruth A. *Made in Czechoslovakia Book 2.* Marietta, Ohio: Antique Publications, 1993.

Giacomini, Mary Jane. *American Bisque Collector's Guide with Prices.* Atglen, Pennsylvania: Schiffer Publishing, 1994

Hall, Doris and Burdell. *Morton Potteries: 99 Years Vol. 2.* Gas City, Indiana: L & W Books, 1995.

Harris, Dee and Jim & Kay Whitaker. *Josef Originals.* Atglen, Pennsylvania: Schiffer Publishing, 1994.

Mangus, Jim and Bev. *An Identification to Shawnee Pottery.* Paducah, Kentucky: Collector Books, 1994.

Newbound, Betty and Bill. *Collector's Encyclopedia of Blue Ridge Dinnerware.* Paducah, Kentucky: Collector Books, 1994.

Newbound, Betty and Bill. *Collector's Encyclopedia of Blue Ridge Dinnerware Volume II.* Paducah, Kentucky: Collector Books, 1998.

Schneider, Mike. *Animal Figures.* Atglen, Pennsylvania: Schiffer Publishing, 1990.

Schneider, Mike. *California Potteries The Complete Book.* Atglen, Pennsylvania: Schiffer Publishing, 1995.

Schneider, Mike. *Royal Copley Identification and Price Guide.* Atglen, Pennsylvania: Schiffer Publishing, 1995.

Stamper, Bernice. *Vallona Starr Ceramics.* Atglen, Pennsylvania: Schiffer Publishing, 1995.

Vanderbilt, Duane and Janice. *The Collector's Guide to Shawnee Pottery.* Paducah, Kentucky: Collector Books, 1992.

Whitaker, Jim and Kaye. *Josef Originals a Second Look.* Atglen, Pennsylvania: Schiffer Publishing, 1996.

White, Carole Bess White. *Collector's Guide to Made in Japan Ceramics.* Paducah, Kentucky: Collector Books, 1994.

Internet

World Book Online, Reference Center, World Book Inc., 2005
web site: http://www.aolsvc.worldbook.aol.com/wb/article

Liberty Blue Dinnerware. Debbie & Randy Coe. Blue and white ironstone dinnerware has been collected for many years, and the introduction of the Liberty Blue pattern in 1975, with its fifteen different historic scenes of colonial America, brought forth keen interest. Color photographs beautifully illustrate all the pieces in a complete set, and interesting facts are given about each historic scene.

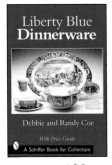

Size: 6" x 9"   95 color photos   128pp.
ISBN: 0-7643-1543-9   soft cover $14.95

Fenton Basket Patterns: Acanthus to Hummingbird. Debbie & Randy Coe. In these two volumes, over 880 known varieties of Fenton baskets are each carefully described, with their individual ware numbers, color, size, decoration, date, and current value, and are individually shown in beautiful color photos. The patterns are presented alphabetically. This volume has the patterns from Acanthus to Hummingbird.

Size: 8 1/2" X 11"   455 color photos   176 pages
                       Price Guide
ISBN: 0-7643-2272-9   hard cover $29.95

Fenton Basket Patterns: Innovation to Wisteria & Numbers. Debbie & Randy Coe. In these two volumes, over 880 known varieties of Fenton baskets are each carefully described, with their individual ware numbers, color, size, decoration, date, and current value, and are individually shown in beautiful color photos. The patterns are presented alphabetically. This volume has the patterns Innovation to Wisteria and the numbered patterns.

Size: 8 1/2" x 11"   440 color photos   176pp.
                       price guide
ISBN: 0-7643-2290-7   hard cover $29.95